My Favorite Seasons

illustrated by Teddy Edinjiklian
written by Dandi

Once, a long, long time ago –
Please don't ask the reasons –
Someone took the whole, wide world
And split it into *seasons*.

7-17-96

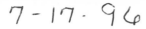

Winter

Spring

Summer

Fall

With the winter comes the snow.
Bundle up from head-to-toe!

White frost puffs when someone talks.

Grown-ups have to shovel walks.

Winter is for snowball fights,
Figure skating, Christmas lights,
Making snowmen, catching flakes,
Happy New Year, frozen lakes.

You will know when winter's through.
Melting snowmen, muddy shoe.
No more frosty Paradise.
No more walking on the ice.

After winter we get spring.
Spring's a time for anything!
Flowers bloom, and so do trees.
Those who are allergic...*sneeze!*

Spring reminds us of a birth.
New life springs up from the earth.
Bears wake up, and robins sing.
Chipmunks go a chittering.

Touch a daisy. Smell a rose!
Shed those bulky winter clothes!

After Easter, play outside.
Is spring best? I can't decide.
Climb a tree with your best friend.
Spring is nearly at an end.

Such bright sunshine rules the day!
Nothing left to do but PLAY!
Summer's here, and spring's all gone.
Parents have to mow the lawn.

Cook-outs, camp-outs, campfires too,
Biking, hiking, swimming, zoo,
Soccer, baseball, tennis, fishing,
Fun is yours just for the wishing!

Hear the crack of baseball bats,
Screaming summer acrobats.
Listen to the nighttime sound.
Chirping cricket songs abound.

Here's a boat if you can row it.
Summer's through before
you know it!

Autumn goes by different names. Some folks call it *Fall*.
If you're into colors, you'll like it best of all.

First the leaves begin to change – orange, red and green.
Add some yellow and you have the perfect autumn scene.

Jump into a pile of leaves.
Listen to the crunch.
Parents have to come with rakes
And rake them in a bunch.

Halloween and pumpkins,
Then Thanksgiving Day.
When those leaves fall off the trees,
The seasons press REPLAY!

Winter, spring, summer, fall, but it's not the end,

Whichever season you like best will come around again!

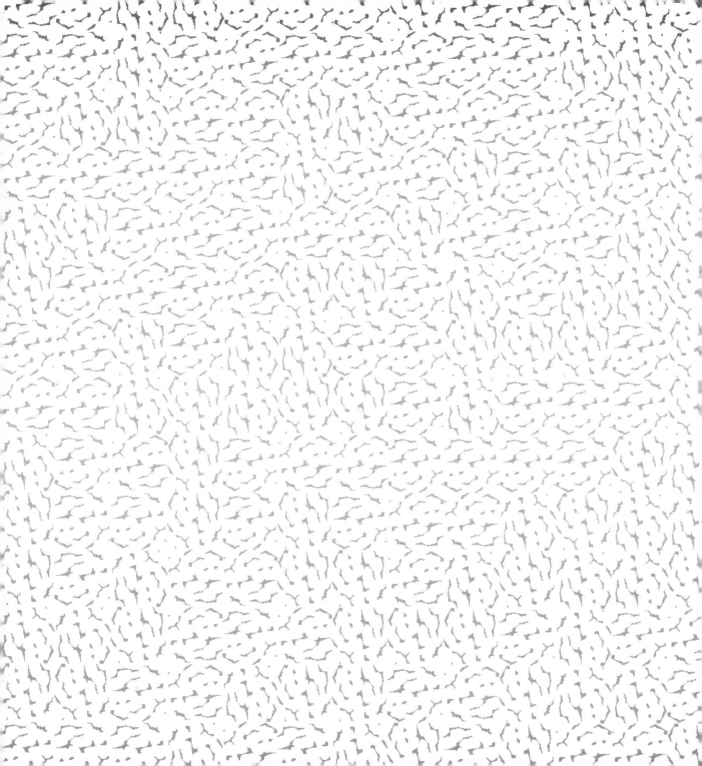